PEAR

True Crime Cases – Volume 1

First edition

This book was professionally typeset on Reedsy.
Find out more at reedsy.com

Contents

One

Edward "Ed" Theodore Gein

Ed Gein was a notorious grave robber and murderer. Some of Hollywood's most notorious villains, such as Norman Bates from "Psycho," were inspired by his antics.

Ed Gein was raised in a strict home by a mother who exercised total control. After she passed away in 1945, his mental state deteriorated.

Investigation of Gein's residence led to the discovery of a seriously disturbed guy who preserved human organs and made garments and accessories out of body parts. Gein was arrested as a suspect in a 1957 murder.

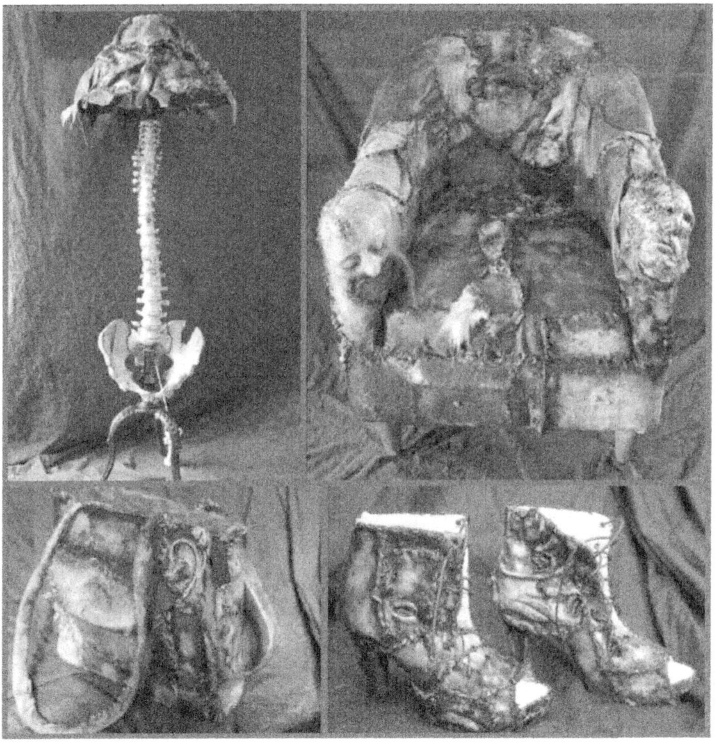

His life was spent in institutions, and the characters Leatherface, Buffalo Bill, and Norman Bates from the films Psycho, The Texas Chainsaw Massacre, and The Silence of the Lambs were all influenced by him.

In La Crosse, Wisconsin, on August 27, 1906, Edward Theodore

Gein was born. Gein was raised in a home where his mother's puritanical sermons on the crimes of lust and carnal desire predominated.

Gein was the son of George, a frightened alcoholic father, and Augusta, a fervently religious mother. Gein had an elder brother named Henry.

Augusta relocated the family to a farm outside of Plainfield, Wisconsin, in 1915. Except for going to school, Gein hardly ever left the farm.

Gein and Henry started working additional odd jobs to support the family when George passed away in 1940. Fire erupted out of control in 1944 on their property when the brothers were burning brush.

Although it was initially thought that Henry had died in the fire, the circumstances of his death and Gein's subsequent actions have led to speculation that the younger brother is to blame.

Gein never left home and was completely dedicated to his mother. But once she passed away in late 1945, he started to spiral out of control.

Now that he was on his own, he kept her room tidy and unaltered while the rest of the house descended into squalor. He also started to become interested in anatomy books.

Despite his strange conduct, Gein was able to sustain himself by working as a handyman and as a babysitter.

Over the years, a few locals from the general vicinity have unexplainably vanished. Mary Hogan, who managed a pub in nearby Pine Grove that Gein sometimes visited, was one of them.

Bernice Worden was reported missing from her Plainfield hardware store on November 16, 1957. The cash register was reportedly taken, and a blood trail could be seen flowing out the rear.

Bernice Worden's son deputy sheriff Frank Worden was suspicious of Ed Gein and Ed was quickly found at a neighbor's home.

The horrifying sight of Worden's headless, gutted body hanging from the ceiling met the officials dispatched to Gein's house that evening.

More disturbing findings were made as the inquiry continued, such as organs in jars and skulls being used as soup bowls.

Gein admitted to killing Worden and Hogan three years prior when being questioned. He also acknowledged committing necrophilia, digging up countless corpses seeking body parts, and making masks and outfits out of skin to wear about the house.

Authorities tried to link him to other deaths and disappearances from the recent past using evidence, but they were unable to come to any firm conclusions.

In January 1958, Gein was declared mentally unable to stand trial after his attorney, William Belter, made a not guilty by reason of insanity plea on his behalf. He was sent to Central State Hospital, where he held several jobs as mason, carpenter's helper, and medical center aide.

Gein was finally found to be competent to stand trial in early 1968. He was convicted of killing Worden that November. He was recommitted to Central State Hospital as a result of the fact that he was also determined to be mad at the time of the murder.

Except for his unsuccessful bid for release in 1974, the mild-mannered Gein made hardly any headlines while incarcerated. Later that decade, when his health began to deteriorate, he was sent to the Mendota Mental Health Institute, where he passed away on July 26, 1984, from cancer and respiratory ailments.

Robert Bloch's 1959 novel Psycho, which Alfred Hitchcock adapted for the big screen the following year, was heavily affected by the tale of Gein's grisly acts, particularly his devotion to a dead mother.

Gein has been mentioned in several songs throughout the years and served as an influence for other infamous movie villains, such as Buffalo Bill (The Silence of the Lambs) and Leatherface (The Texas Chainsaw Massacre).

Two

Richard Trenton Chase (The Vampire Killer of Sacramento)

Due to his practice of cannibalism and drinking the blood of his victims, Richard Trenton Chase earned the nickname "The Vampire Killer of Sacramento." Chase killed six people.

In Sacramento, California, on May 23, 1950, Chase was born. He was known to abuse animals, wet the bed, and start fires when he was younger. As he grew older, he began to consume alcohol and use drugs, primarily marijuana and LSD.

He spent a large portion of his life going in and out of mental hospitals. Because of his drug and alcohol misuse, he acquired hypochondria. Which led him to tell medical professionals that his pulmonary artery had been stolen, his heart stopped pumping, and that his blood was turning to powder.

He moved into an apartment on his own when he was 21. He eventually had to go back home since his housemates had had enough of him and wanted to leave. His father raised rent for a new apartment, so he didn't stay for very long in his old apartment. He had no girlfriends and no social life. Chase used to hunt and kill animals, then consume them raw or mixed.

He used the blood from a rabbit he slaughtered to inject himself, which resulted in blood poisoning that required hospitalization in 1976. He terrified many patients and staff, who referred to him as Dracula.

He frequently had blood on his face, which he said was the result of cutting himself while shaving. He was actually draining the blood out of birds by chewing off their heads. He was discharged after he started taking his medication.

Chase was discovered in a field close to Lake Tahoe, Nevada, a year later. He was bloodied from a cow and nude. Despite reporting the occurrence, nothing further was done. A few months later, Chase killed Ambrose Griffin with a single shot. The FBI claimed that the incident was a drive-by shooting. At first, nobody recognized Chase as the shooter.

Terry Wallin, David Wallin's pregnant 22-year-old wife, was his next victim. When her husband got home from work, he discovered her disemboweled and blood-drained. Chase looked to have gathered her blood and placed it in a yogurt cup for drinking.

Once more, Chase was not shown to be the brutal killer. As a result of the investigation, further events were identified, including the break-in of a nearby home where the dismembered remains of a dog were discovered.

Based on the facts, the FBI created a suspect profile that was a perfect fit for Chase. The FBI requested any information that may help in his capture, but another murder was soon committed.

When a neighbor went into Evelyn Miroth's house, they discovered someone slaughtered. Not only was Evelyn, 36, found dead, but also her 6-year-old son Jason and a family friend named Daniel Meredith. Michael Ferreira, Evelyn's nephew who was 22 months old, was also absent from the house.

It was thought that Michael was also slain and the suspect

carried the body with him when he fled because the playpen where he would typically be located was covered in blood and contained a cushion with a gunshot hole.

A woman in her 20s gave the police a crucial tip when she claimed to have run into a high school classmate who had approached her car. He was quite skinny and had blood stains on his sweatshirt, and she observed that his eyes were sunken.

He was Richard Trenton Chase, according to her. He lived within a mile of most of the crime scenes, the police learned. Police surrounded Chase's flat and detained him. He was arrested forcibly, and a gun discovered in evidence was connected to every murder.

Authorities also found three blenders that had blood, a 12-inch butcher knife, rubber boots, animal collars, and various plates inside the refrigerator that contained body parts. Even a calendar with the word "today" marked on the days of the Wallin and Miroth killings was discovered in his flat. A headless, mummified baby was later discovered in a box outside of a deserted lot. It was determined that it was Evelyn Miroth's nephew.

Chase entered a not guilty plea on the grounds of insanity as the trials got underway in 1979. He was convicted guilty of all six murder charges despite being judged legally sane at the time of the offenses. Chase acknowledged during an interview that he had gone door-checking while strolling the streets. If the door was locked, he said, "it meant you weren't welcome."

He started taking medication after his conviction. He accumulated the medication till he had enough to commit himself rather than actually taking it. In his cell, he was discovered dead in December 1979.

Three

Edmund Kemper (The Co-ed Killer)

Edmund Kemper III was a giant, both as a newborn and as a boy. (He'll eventually become a 300-pound, 6-foot-9-inch "hulk" of a guy.)

When Edmund is nine years old, his parents divorced, leaving him with his mother, Clarnell and his two sisters. Clarnell frequently makes fun of Edmund's stature and his "weirdo" demeanor. She keeps telling him that no lady will ever fall in love with him.

He is taught to detest himself, but he also picks up a hatred for everyone else, particularly women.

Early on, his perverted desires are obvious. His sister makes fun of him for being attracted to a female teacher and queries why he doesn't try to kiss her.

He answers...

"I'd have to kill her first if I kissed her,"

Playing the role of someone who is being executed in a gas chamber is one of his favorite school games. He first beheads his sister's doll at home before killing his animals. Edmund, age 10, buries his cat alive.

He digs it up when it has died, decapitates it, and then displays it on a spike. His first trophy is this one.

At age 13, he attacks the substitute cat with a machete. He holds onto its leg as he chops off the top of its skull, getting covered in blood as he does so. According to author Harold Schechter, "animal torture isn't a step" for serial killers. It's a practice.

Edmund had fantasies of killing everyone in the village and having sex with their bodies during puberty.

His mother confines him to the cellar out of concern that he may rape his sister. Edmund tries to make amends with his father at the age of 15.

Edmund is forced to live with his grandparents on their ranch in California after being rejected by his father once more. He shoots his grandma in the head during his first summer there before brutally stabbing her because...

I was simply considering how it could feel to kill Grandma.

Edmund kills his grandfather by shooting him when he came back. Later, Edmund claims that he killed him so that he (the grandfather) wouldn't have to witness what he (Edmund) had done to the man's wife.

While waiting for them, Edmund calls his mother and the police.

He is admitted to State the Hospital after being identified as a paranoid schizophrenic. He enjoys listening to serial rapists recount their atrocities.

He presents a calm exterior while harboring a fixation with sexual violence. His exceptionally high IQ is demonstrated through tests. And after just five years, he receives parole.

His doctor and Edmund both advise against doing this. (They give him back to his mother, without irony.) Eight ladies will now perish.

Edmund Kemper receives nothing in the way of mental health assistance or psychiatric examinations despite having killed two people, except from one evaluation by a panel of psychiatrists following his parole.

The panel expunges his juvenile record because they think he has changed.

But he had slain the day before the hearing. And after his release, he killed three times.

He specifically targets female hitchhikers. (Many of them hold college degrees; thus he was nicknamed, "The Co-Ed killer"). He swiftly killed them using a knife or a.22-caliber pistol he purchased.

Since his perversion doesn't require pain, death usually comes quickly. Instead, he transports their corpses to his house so he can have the time and room he requires.

His necrophilia entails taking pictures of the corpse and then having sex with it. He engages in sexual activity with the head and the viscera after being dissected and beheaded.

He kills his victim twice, then uses the meat in a macaroni casserole.

Later, he wraps the corpses in bags and buries them, but he throws the heads into a ravine. In order to minimize forensic evidence, he takes care to remove the bullet if he has shot them. Before Kemper encounters his mother, the primary event, six women pass away in this manner.

With a knife and a hammer, Kemper storms into his mother's bedroom just before Easter 1973. He fractures her skull, removes her head, and engages in sexual activity with the body parts. Then...

He forced her larynx down the garbage disposal, which instantly spat it back out into his face. This was one of the more symbolically significant crimes in the annals of criminal wickedness.

" As much as she had complained, raged, and screamed at me for so many years, Kemper would later tell the authorities, "That seemed appropriate."

Kemper uses her remaining skull as a dartboard after that, propped up against the fireplace. Later, he extends a dinner invitation to the close friend of his mother. He uses a scarf to choke her and then spends the entire night abusing her body.

Edmund Kemper runs away. When he arrives in Colorado, he realizes that all is finished because his mother was killed. Practically speaking, there is little likelihood that he won't be connected to this murder.

He then calls the Santa Cruz police and confesses over the phone. Until one of them makes the decision to come out and arrest him, Kemper waits calmly by the phone. His admission persuades them.

Kemper admits to being insane, but at his trial, just like during his previous psychiatrist visit, he was deemed legally sane.

He is found guilty on eight charges of murder after three weeks. The court queries Kemper as to what he believes would be a just penalty for his offenses.

Death via torture, Kemper responds. Instead, he is given 8 life sentences and transferred for observation to the California Medical Facility State Prison.

Four

John Wayne Gacy

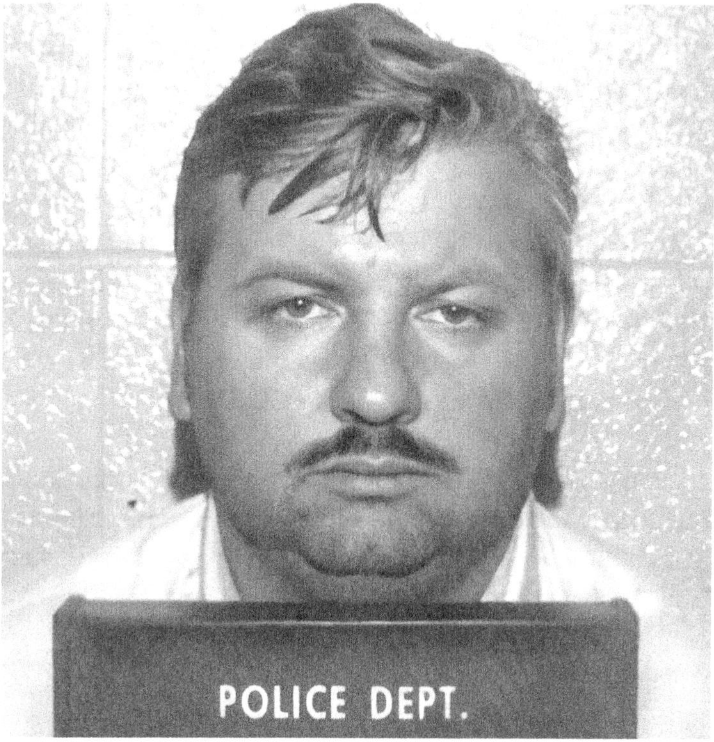

John Wayne Gacy confesses to killing around twenty youths, young men and burying their bodies under his suburban Chicago home on December 22, 1978.

Gacy was awarded the death penalty in March 1980 after being found guilty of 33 sex-related killings that occurred between 1972 and 1978.

Gacy was born on March 17, 1942, in Chicago. On the outside, he seemed to have a fairly typical middle-class upbringing, but according to some reports, Gacy had a violent, alcoholic father and health problems as a young child.

After getting hitched in 1964, Gacy relocated to Iowa with his bride to take over the management of his father-in-Kentucky law's Fried Chicken eateries.

Two kids were born to the couple. However, after Gacy was accused of sexually assaulting one of his male employees in 1968, his wife decided to end their marriage. He was given a 10-year prison term, but after serving only a portion of it owing to good behavior, he was allowed to go.

Back in Chicago, Gacy established a contracting business and remarried. The ostensibly respectable businessman, engaged in local politics and once posed for a picture with the first lady Rosalynn Carter, was actually a sexual predator who led a double life.

In 1972, he committed his first homicide. Male prostitutes and young employees of Gacy's business were among his victims.

Usually, he used enticements to draw his victims back to his house, where he would deceive them into becoming shackled or having a rope placed around their necks.

He would then use chloroform to put them to sleep before raping, torturing, and killing them. Gacy's atrocities went unnoticed at first because he was a well-known community figure who occasionally disguised up as a clown to amuse ill children.

Robert Piest's disappearance in December 1978 led to the discovery that the teen was last seen with Gacy, which raised suspicions about the serial killer. Police searched Gacy's Norwood Park residence after becoming aware of his Iowa sex crime conviction. When they initially smelled a foul smell emanating from a crawl area, they assumed it was coming from a broken sewage line.

Later, other evidence, including a store receipt, that connected Gacy to Piest and other young men who had been reported missing were discovered at his residence.

Investigators found 29 bodies buried on Gacy's property after he admitted to the crime, along with four additional that he had thrown in surrounding rivers after he ran out of space at home.

Gacy served 14 years on Death Row following his conviction, during which time he painted clowns and other figures that were sold for thousands of dollars each.

The 52-year-old Gacy, also known as the Killer Clown by the media, was executed by lethal injection at the Stateville Penitentiary in Joliet, Illinois, on May 10, 1994, after exhausting all of his appeals.

Five

H. H. Holmes

H.H. Holmes, also known as Herman Mudgett, was an American con artist and confidence trickster who is largely regarded as the nation's first identified serial killer. He was born May 16, 1861? in Gilmanton, New Hampshire, and died May 7, 1896 in Philadelphia, Pennsylvania.

Mudgett was born into a prosperous family and demonstrated cognitive traits at a young age. He supposedly caught animals and operated on them; some stories of his life even imply that he killed a little playmate.

He was always interested in medicine. Mudgett was an average student in medical school at the University of Michigan. When a widowed hairdresser accused him of making a fraudulent promise of marriage to her in 1884, he almost lost the opportunity to graduate.

Mudgett relocated to Chicago in 1886, where he was employed as a pharmacist under the name "Dr. H.H. Holmes." Shortly after, he allegedly started murdering people in order to steal their possessions. He created "Murder Castle," a home for himself that featured soundproof rooms, trapdoors, secret passages, and doors that could be closed from the outside.

Gas jets were also installed to asphyxiate victims, and a kiln was used to burn the bodies. During the World's Columbian Exposition in Chicago in 1893, when he is said to have been at the height of his power, he allegedly seduced and murdered a number of women, usually by being engaged to them and killing them after taking possession of their life savings.

Mudgett also mandated that his staff members carry life insurance policies with him listed as the beneficiary so that he might get the proceeds in the event that they were killed. Many of his victims' bodies were sold to nearby medical colleges by him.

Following a house fire in 1893, Mudgett was detained for insurance fraud but was soon freed. He then devised a plan with a friend named Ben Pitezel to swindle an insurance provider by fabricating Pitezel's passing.

Pitezel and Mudgett proceeded to Colorado, Missouri, New

York, Pennsylvania, Tennessee, and Texas after buying a $10,000 life insurance policy, where they carried out additional fraud (along the way, Mudgett also married).

Mudgett was detained for a short time in St. Louis after arriving in Missouri and being accused of fraud. He met career criminal Marion Hedgepeth while he was incarcerated, and she agreed to assist Mudgett in his insurance scam with Pitezel. Pitezel in the meantime, relocated to Philadelphia and set up a phony patent office to con inventors.

Mudgett killed Pitezel in Philadelphia after being let out of jail. Pitezel's widow, who was aware of her husband's involvement in the insurance plan, was then persuaded by Mudgett that her husband was still alive. He later gave her $500 of the money he had amassed.

Mudgett murdered three of Pitezel's five kids out of fear that they might call the police. Hedgepeth informed insurance inspectors of the fraud, and Mudgett was apprehended in Boston, Massachusetts, in 1894. He was found guilty of killing Pitezel and given a hanging verdict in Philadelphia.

Although some experts believe that the actual number was more than 200, Mudgett admitted to 27 murders (he later boosted the amount to more than 130). For $10,000, Mudgett sold the Hearst Corporation his story.

Six

Ted Bundy

Ted Bundy was a charming, articulate, and intellectual young man when he was born on November 24, 1946, in Burlington, Vermont. However, Bundy had showed glimpses of the vicious serial killer he would become while he was a teenager living in Washington.

In interviews, he recounted being antisocial and prowling the streets in search of abandoned pieces of pornography or windows that were left open so he could see unsuspecting women; he also had a long history of thievery as a child that was eventually expunged when he was 18 years old.

He had completed college by 1972 and had excellent promise for a career in law or politics. However, that profession would be cut short when he found his true calling and brutally attacked his first known victim in 1974.

In Washington, initially close to his home, he would prey on young, attractive college women. From there, he would travel east to Utah, Colorado, and finally Florida. Bundy would utilize a deception to prey on these women, frequently strolling on crutches while sporting a sling on his arm or a phony cast on his leg.

He would then persuade his victims to assist him in carrying books or unloading items from his car using his charm and a phony infirmity.

He was also well-known for pretending to be authorities like police officers or firefighters in order to win the trust of his victims before attacking. He would use a crowbar or pipe to hit them over the head as soon as they arrived to his 1968 tan Volkswagen Beetle.

After striking his victims, he would bind them, render them helpless, and push them into the car. To keep his victim hidden as he was being driven away, Bundy frequently removed the passenger seat and stowed it in the trunk or backseat.

This allowed Bundy to rape and kill a large number of women. He frequently beat or strangled his victims before mutilating them after they passed away. Then, to get further sexual enjoyment, he continued to visit the corpses at their disposal locations or even took them home.

He even cruelly displayed their severed heads in his residence in certain instances, and slept next to their bodies until the putrefaction made it intolerable.

Numerous people got in touch with authorities to report Bundy as a possible matching suspect as death counts increased and witness descriptions spread.

However, despite his appearing good character and neat look, cops constantly disqualified him. He figured out how to leave almost no forensically detectable evidence, which allowed him to evade capture for an even longer period of time.

On August 16, 1975, in Utah, Bundy was ultimately apprehended for the first time after eluding a patrol cruiser. Masks, handcuffs, rope, and other sinister objects were found during the vehicle search, but there was no concrete evidence connecting him to the crimes.

He was freed but kept under close observation until several

months later, when he was apprehended once more for the kidnapping and assault of one of his victims. After being moved from Utah to Colorado for a new trial, Bundy escaped custody a year later but was quickly apprehended.

On December 30, 1977, he was able to escape a second time, making it to Florida where he continued his killing rampage. Before being arrested once more for a driving infraction on February 15, 1978, he raped or killed at least six more victims, five of whom were Florida State University students.

On January 24, 1989, he ultimately received a death sentence and passed away in the electric chair. Although Bundy admitted to 30 killings at the time of his death, the precise number of his victims is still unknown.

Seven

Rodney Alcala

1943 saw the birth of Rodney Alcala in San Antonio, Texas. When Alcala was eight years old, his father relocated the family to Mexico, only to leave them there three years later. Then, his mother relocated Alcala and his sister to a Los Angeles suburb.

Alcala enlisted in the Army as a clerk at the age of 17, but after having a nervous breakdown, he was medically discharged for having mental health problems.

The bright young man went on to UCLA after having an IQ of 135. He wouldn't, however, stay there for very long.

Rodney Alcala had a signature style, like many serial killers.

His hallmark attacks included beating, biting, raping, and strangling (frequently choking victims until they fell unconscious, then starting the act over again when they woke up).

Only two of these things was he effective at on his first documented attempt at killing. Tali Shapiro, an eight-year-old girl he enticed into his Hollywood apartment in 1968, was the victim.

Shapiro barely made it through her rape and assault; she was saved by a bystander who had called the police with a tip about a probable kidnapping. When the police arrived at his flat, Alcala ran away and eluded capture for years.

He relocated to New York and, paradoxically, studied under Roman Polanski while attending New York University's film program under the alias John Berger.

Alcala was eventually recognized as the person responsible for Tali Shapiro's rape and attempted murder owing to an FBI poster.

He was detained in 1971 but only charged with assault and sentenced to prison (Shapiro's family prevented her from testifying, making a conviction for rape impossible). He first served three years in prison before being sentenced to another two years for assaulting a 13-year-old girl.

Sadly, the authorities then allowed Alcala to visit relatives in New York. Investigators now think that he killed college student Elaine Hover, who was the goddaughter of both Sammy Davis Jr. and Dean Martin and the daughter of a well-known Hollywood nightclub owner, within seven days of his arrival there.

Soon after all of this, in 1978, Alcala managed to work as a typesetter for the Los Angeles Times using his real identity, which was now associated with a significant criminal history.

He worked as a typewriter during the day and recruited young females for his professional photography portfolio at night, some of whom he never heard from again.

Liane Leedom, then 17 years old, was fortunate enough to emerge unscathed from a photo shoot with Rodney Alcala the year following her appearance on the Dating Game.

She recalled how he "showed her his portfolio, which in addition to shots of women included spread after spread of [naked] teenage boys."

The lawsuit involving 12-year-old Robin Samsoe was the one that ultimately brought an end to Rodney Alcala's murderous rampage. On June 20, 1979, she vanished while she was leaving Huntington Beach, California, for dance class.

Samsoe's friends claimed that while they were on the beach, a stranger approached them and inquired about participating in a picture session. They declined, so Samsoe departed and quickly rode a friend's bike to the ballet.

Between the beach and class, Samsoe vanished at some point. Her animal-ravaged bones were discovered in a wooded location close to the Pasadena foothills of the Sierra Madre about 12 days later by a park ranger.

A police sketch artist created a composite after questioning Samsoe's pals, and Alcala's previous parole officer recognized the face in it. Police were sure they had Alcala thanks to the sketch, his criminal history, and the discovery of Samsoe's earrings in Alcala's Seattle storage locker.

The jury in Alcala's 2010 trial found him guilty of the four DNA-backed counts as well as the murder of Samsoe.

Tali Shapiro, the young woman Alcala raped and battered approximately 40 years prior, was a surprise witness at his sentencing.

Shapiro was present to see that justice had been served for Jill

Parenteau, 21, Robin Samsoe, 12, Jill Barcomb, 18, Georgia Wixted, 27, and Charlotte Lamb. For the third time, the death penalty was again imposed on Alcala.

The "Dating Game Killer" has been connected to numerous other cold case murders after that trial, including two for which he entered a guilty plea in New York in 2013.

Before he was given the death penalty, Rodney is said to have murdered more than 130 people, including a nurse, a flight attendant, a pianist who aspired to attend medical school, and a number of young girls.

Rodney Alcala passed away on July 24, 2021, at the age of 77 due to natural causes while still incarcerated in California on death row.

Eight

The Zodiac Killer

Unknown American serial killer known as the "Zodiac Killer" is suspected of killing at least five persons in northern California between 1968 and 1969. Another crime that has been connected to the Zodiac killer is the 1966 stabbing death of an 18-year-old college student in Riverside, California.

The case served as the basis for the renowned Clint Eastwood-starring action movie Dirty Harry from 1971, as well as the critically praised David Fincher thriller Zodiac (2007).

In a lonely location north of San Francisco, a young couple was shot and killed in 1968. The following year, another couple was attacked in a similar manner, although this time the male victim lived.

In order to inform them of the crime and confess to the 1968 killings, the murderer called the police after the 1969 attack. Another young couple was attacked by the Zodiac killer later that year, but this time only the man survived. A taxi driver who was the final victim was shot in October 1969.

Because of the killer's mocking letters to newspapers and phone calls to police, the murders received extensive investigation and media coverage. His letters from 1969 to 1974 included four ciphers or cryptograms, the first of which was sent in three sections to three Bay Area newspapers in July 1969.

His messages were signed with a symbol like the crosshairs of a gunsight and frequently began, "this is the Zodiac speaking." The "408 cipher," so called because of the amount of characters it contained, was quickly cracked by two private individuals.

The "340 cipher," which was sent to the San Francisco Chronicle in November 1969 and was finally cracked in 2020 by a group of three amateur codebreakers. The 340 cipher began with the words "I hope you are having lots of fun in trying to catch me." Another cipher read in part, "I like killing people because it is so much fun," was also sent to the newspaper in that month.

The Zodiac case still has many unanswered questions. Although this claim is debatable, crime writer Robert Graysmith asserted that the Zodiac killer continued to commit murders well into the 1980s.

Several detectives claimed to have identified the Zodiac killer during the 1990s; the most popular suspect was Arthur Leigh Allen (1933–1992), a teacher from Vallejo, California, who had been institutionalized in 1975 for child molestation, though his association with the Zodiac killer has never been proven.

Nine

Jack The Ripper

Unknown as a serial killer, Jack the Ripper is believed to have operated in and around London's Whitechapel neighborhood in the early 1888s in the majority of its impoverished neighborhoods.

Both in the criminal case files and the contemporaneous journalistic sources, the murderer was referred to as the Whitechapel Murderer and Leather Apron.

Attacks ascribed to Jack the Ripper frequently targeted female prostitutes who resided and worked in the East End of London's slums; these victims typically had their necks severed before undergoing stomach mutilations.

At least three of the victims had internal organs removed, which suggested that the murderer may have had some surgical or anatomical training.

More persistent rumors relating the killings surfaced in September and October 1888. Scotland Yard and the media both received letters from someone or some persons claiming to be the culprit.

The phrase "Jack the Ripper" was first used in a letter that was allegedly written by the murderer and publicized in the media. The letter was a hoax, and it may have been made by journalists to increase interest in the topic and readership for their publications.

The "From Hell" letter that George Lusk of the Whitechapel Vigilance Committee received was accompanied by a portion of a preserved human kidney that was purportedly stolen from one of the victims.

The sheer severity of the murders and the way the media covered them contributed to the public's growing belief in a single serial killer known as "Jack the Ripper."

Due to widespread newspaper coverage, The Ripper experienced significant and ongoing global recognition, and the myths expanded. Any of the eleven violent homicides that took place in Whitechapel between 1888 and 1891 could not be conclusively linked by the police to the killings that year.

Mary Ann Nichols, Annie Chapman, Elizabeth Stride, Catherine Eddowes, and Mary Jane Kelly are known as the "canonical five." It is commonly believed that their murders between August 31 and November 9, 1888, are most likely connected.

Folklore, pseudohistory, and true historical facts have all been incorporated into the legends that have developed around the murders because they were never solved.

There are presently more than a hundred theories about who the real Jack the Ripper is, and the study and research of the Jack the Ripper cases is referred to as "ripperology." The murders have inspired countless fictional works.

Ten

Joachim Kroll

Joachim Kroll terrorized western Germany between 1955 and 1976 by committing some of the most insane acts ever. He committed at least fourteen murders and several rapes.

It was obvious that the victims had been slain, and that a cannibal had also committed the murders. Slices from the victims' bodies were taken in a way that suggested the killer planned to consume some of the corpses.

Kroll, who was born in 1933, was the eighth and youngest child.

He was regarded by those in his neighborhood as a weak child. Additionally, he frequently soiled the bed as a child, which was incredibly embarrassing.

The effects of World War II on Germany caused his family to experience famine and destitution. During World War II, his father was a POW in Russia, which was unpleasant and embarrassing for the family.

Kroll found it difficult to engage in meaningful conversation with women his own age because he felt insufficient sexually. This most likely had a significant impact on his decision to use rape to satiate his sexual needs.

After his mother passed away in 1955, Kroll soon committed his first murder. We will never know if the date was coincidental, but it is still worth mentioning as a timeline.

Kroll committed rape and murder by stabbing, mutilating, cannibalizing, and strangling among other crimes. When the bodies of the victims were discovered, it was evident that significant portions of the buttocks, thighs, and belly had been sliced and removed in preparation for consumption.

Except for one elderly woman, almost all of his victims were young. Except for the one Kroll killed while attempting to rape his fiancée, they were all women. Before being slain, every victim was raped.

Kroll's actions resulted in more harm than just the heinous killing of people. To prevent being implicated in some of Kroll's murders and even being arrested for them, numerous other men committed murder themselves.

As a result of Kroll's inability to control his boasting when being interrogated by the police, authorities only know what he told them.

Marion Kettner, a four-year-old girl, was Kroll's last victim. Police canvassed adjacent homes after receiving a report that she was missing from a playground.

"A plumber swiftly confirmed a witness reports," The report read that "Kroll had told him that the upstairs toilet in their apartment building was clogged 'with guts'."

When police arrived to do their investigation, they saw Kroll frying the body of young Marion. He was taken into custody right away.

He acknowledged to thirteen killings and one attempted murder, but was only given a sentence for nine because several of the others were already crimes for which he had received convictions.

Kroll was handed nine consecutive life terms, and he passed away from a heart attack in jail in 1991.

Eleven

Gary Ridgway (The Green River Killer)

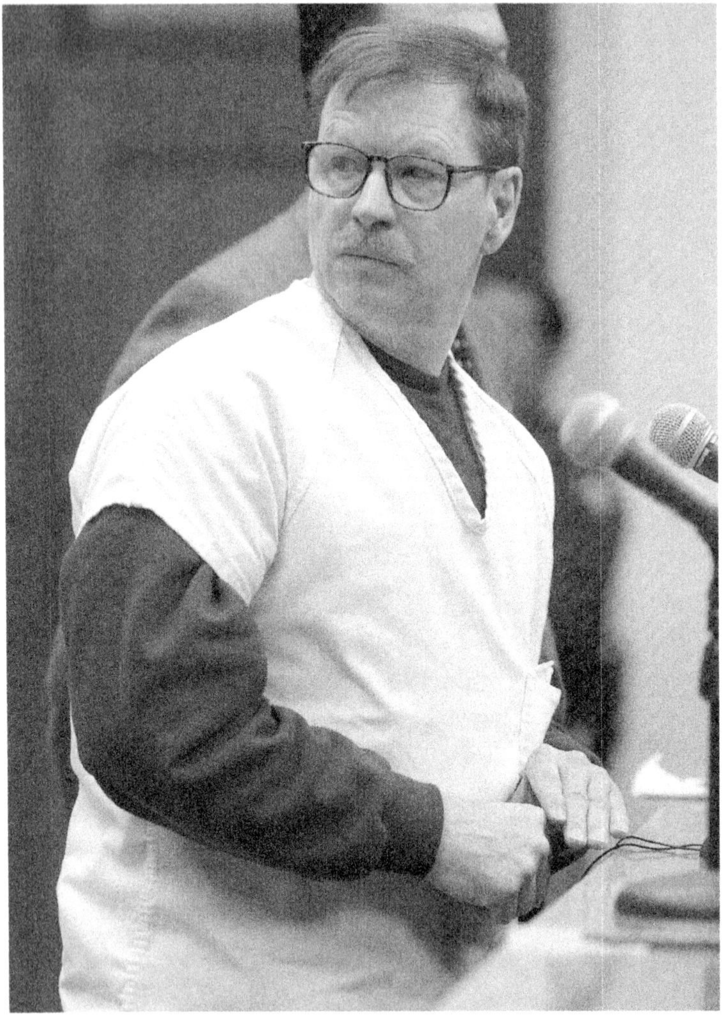

Gary Ridgway, full name Gary Leon Ridgway, alias Green River Killer, was an American criminal and the deadliest convicted serial killer in the nation.

He was born in Salt Lake City, Utah, on February 18, 1949. Although he admitted to just 48 deaths in 2003, he claimed to have slain up to 80 women in Washington during the 1980s and 1990s, many of whom were prostitutes.

In the area of Washington that is now SeaTac, Ridgway grew up. His mother worked as a salesperson and his father as a bus driver. Later, the younger Ridgway alleged that his mother had acted improperly.

Notably, he claimed that mother would wash his genitalia after he wet the bed, a custom that remained until his early teens.

He eventually started having murderous fantasies, and in the middle of the 1960s, he stabbed a small boy. Ridgway enlisted in the U.S. Navy for two years after receiving his high school diploma in 1969, at the age of 20, and then relocated in the Seattle region, where he worked as a truck painter. He had three marriages over the subsequent 30 years, giving birth to a son.

Ridgway was detained in 1980 for reportedly choking a prostitute, but no charges were brought against him because he claimed she bit him. He was taken into custody for solicitation two years later.

Shortly after, Ridgway is thought to have started his murdering spree. It was believed that a 16-year-old girl who vanished after leaving her foster home in July 1982 was his first victim.

A week later, the Green River held her body. More than 40

women, many of whom were prostitutes or fugitives, were raped and murdered by Ridgway over the course of the next two years.

The epithet "Green River Killer" came about because several of Ridgway's early victims were eventually located in or close to the river; other bodies were found in isolated woodland regions. He killed more people after 1984, with the most recent killing taking place in 1998.

Police eventually created a special task team in August 1982 after coming to the conclusion that a serial killer was at large. Ridgway quickly turned into a suspect.

He was investigated in 1983 over the disappearance of a prostitute who a witness said had entered his truck. In 1984, Ridgway passed a polygraph test and refuted the accusations.

Detectives eventually came upon a report from 1982 that described Ridgway being found by police with a prostitute in a parked car; two years later, a body was recovered nearby.

Authorities secured a search warrant for Ridgway's residence and place of business in 1987. But none of the objects, not even carpet fibers or ropes, could be connected to the victims.

A DNA sample was also acquired from Ridgway, but it was unable to be matched with the semen found in the bodies due to the state of technology at the time.

But in 2001, a match was found thanks to the development of

more sophisticated tests, and Ridgway was taken into custody later that year.

Ridgway originally claimed to be innocent, but he quickly admitted to the crimes and said he had intended to kill as many prostitutes as he could. He chose sex workers because he "hated" most of them and because he believed they might not be reported missing.

He agreed to a plea agreement in 2003, and as a result, he was given 48 consecutive life sentences without the possibility of release.

He also consented to divulge the locations of undiscovered bodies. Many people believed he was responsible for more fatalities, but in 2013, Ridgway claimed he had killed over 80 women.

Twelve

Frederick (Fred) West

In order to fulfill his sexual desires, West and his wife Rose preyed on impressionable young girls and women, which ultimately led to murder.

The builder, who was born in 1941 into a Herefordshire farm laboring family, emigrated to Gloucester in 1962.

When Rose was 18 years old, he married her in 1972. Since she was 15, the two had been having an affair, and this was his second marriage.

His first union was with Catherine Costello, also called Rena, who was 18 at the time and carrying another man's kid.

In 1963, she gave birth to a daughter named Charmaine, and in 1964, West's daughter Anne Marie was born.

West's children's nanny in 1967, Anne McFall, who is believed to be West's first victim, resided with him in his trailer. He would begin his horrific killing spree with her.

As a result of allegations of sexual assault and violence, Ms. Costello left West in 1969, and her friends and family lost touch with her in 1971. Later, West acknowledged killing her in 1994.

Over a 20-year span, from 1967 to 1987, West and his wife tortured, raped, and killed an undetermined number of women.

There are 12 known victims; the pair is accused with 10 killings collectively, and Fred West is accused of two additional deaths.

In July 1967, Anne McFall, then 18 years old and carrying West's child, vanished. In June 1994, her remains and those of her unborn child were discovered in a field at Kempley, which is close to West's hometown of Much Marcle in Herefordshire.

The 26-year-old Ms. Costello's body was also discovered nearby.

While Rose West was serving time for stealing car tires and a vehicle tax disc in 1971, Ms. Costello's eight-year-old daughter was murdered. On 1994, her body was discovered at their former house in Midland Road, Gloucester.

At their city residence on Cromwell Street, the graves of Lynda Gough, 19, Carole Ann Cooper, 15, Lucy Partington, 21, Therese Sigenthaler, 21, Shirley Hubbard, 15, Juanita Mott, 18, Shirley Ann Robinson, 18, and Alison Chambers, 17, were all discovered.

Heather, the couple's 16-year-old daughter, was also discovered dead at the house. Despite giving conflicting explanations, her parents had never reported her missing.

In 1992, an inquiry was launched as a result of an accidental interaction between a group of school children and a police officer in Gloucester.

Detective Con Hazel Savage discovered the Wests' murderous trail after learning of a "family joke" the children had told social workers about the couple's missing daughter being "under the patio."

Eventually, Detective Con Savage persuaded senior officers that it was possible the "joke" wasn't just dark humor, and it was Heather's disappearance that led police to Cromwell Street.

West acknowledged killing his daughter in 1994.

The admission would direct authorities to the Wests' "home of horrors," where they discovered nine young women's bodies—including the daughter of the suspect—buried in the basement or garden.

The first remains discovered were those of Heather. As authorities continued to uncover more bodies, the lower portion of the house was practically destroyed during the search.

The route then took them to Much Marcle, where West was born, before continuing to the neighboring Midland Road.

West was accused of 12 murders, but before going to trial, at the age of 53, he hanged himself in his remand cell, leaving his wife to face the legal system alone.

When Rose was imprisoned that year for the murder of 10 young girls and women, she rose to become one of the most infamous female mass murderers in Britain.

Mr. Justice Mantell, the trial judge, expressed his desire for Rose never to be freed.

In 1996, the house owned by the Wests on Cromwell Street was demolished and a garden and footpath were built in its stead.

Thirteen

Andrei Chikatilo (The Soviet Ripper)

Andrei Chikatilo, full name Andrei Romanovich Chikatilo, often known as the Rostov Ripper, was a Soviet serial murderer who killed at least 50 people between 1978 and 1990.

He was born on October 16, 1936, in Yablochnoye, USSR (now Ukraine), and passed away on February 14, 1994, in Moscow, Russia.

In addition to the enormous number of victims, his case is notable because Soviet authorities were unable to warn the public during their investigation due to the official ideology of the nation, which held that serial killing was impossible in a socialist society.

Chikatilo grew up following the great Ukrainian famine of the 1930s, which resulted in millions of deaths and saw many turn to cannibalism in order to live.

His mother would frequently remind him as a child that he had an older sibling who had been abducted and eaten by neighbors.

Chikatilo appears to have been inspired by the unprovable myth to cannibalize some of his victims. Chikatilo was a voracious reader who took a special interest in tales that detailed the treatment of German prisoners by Soviet captors during World War II.

Chikatilo married in 1963 and worked as a telephone engineer in the area of Rostov-na-Donu after finishing his military service.

He graduated from Rostov Liberal Arts University in 1971, after which he entered the teaching profession. However, he was forced to leave his position after some parents accused Chikatilo of sexually assaulting their kids.

Chikatilo started killing people in 1978, preying on young people he met in Rostov-na-train Donu's stations and bus stops, as well as other towns he traveled to for his numerous professions.

The authorities quickly realized a serial murderer was operating in the area since all the victims had distinctive mutilations.

Nevertheless, Chikatilo was able to avoid capture for many years, in part because his crimes took advantage of flaws in the crumbling Soviet Union's social structure.

Young people who lived in poverty were eager to move to the city, but because they frequently had no friends or contacts there and little money, they were easily seduced and their disappearances frequently went unreported.

Chikatilo was detained by a policeman in 1984 after the officer saw him sexually assaulting a girl at a train station.

Police misread the man's blood type, which tests revealed did not correspond to the type suggested by semen discovered at one of the crime locations. Despite the fact that the briefcase he was carrying was discovered to contain a long knife and other suspicious objects.

After that, Chikatilo was accused with stealing supplies from a former employer and given a one-year prison term, though he was released after three months.

Following his release, Chikatilo resumed killing, prompting a thorough police investigation that included round-the-clock monitoring of a district's bus and train stations.

He was recognized as the primary suspect in the crimes and taken into custody in 1990; at the time of his arrest, he was in possession of a briefcase with materials that were still in it when he was taken into custody six years prior.

Chikatilo confessed while in detention. He was taken there after showing police his techniques at numerous crime scenes.

He was executed in a Moscow prison after being convicted of 52 murders and given the death penalty. In 1995, Citizen X, a television film based on Chikatilo's life, premiered.

Fourteen

Jeffrey Dahmer

Jeffrey Dahmer, one of the most renowned serial killers in American history, was born and grew up in Bath Township,

Ohio, an affluent neighborhood of Akron.

Although much has been said about his childhood habits, including instances of animal brutality, he seemed to be a typical child at least on the surface.

He always had a job that paid well as an adult, and his coworkers thought he was quiet and courteous. He was living alone in a tiny one-bedroom apartment and working at a chocolate factory in Milwaukee at the time of his arrest.

On July 22, 1991, a young guy exited his flat and flagged down a police cruiser, prompting a search of Dahmer's home. The bones of 11 young males, the most of whom were black, Hispanic, or Asian, were found in the apartment.

Dahmer admitted that he had cooked and consumed some of the dismembered body parts after the bodies had been torn apart. When asked why he did such horrifying things, Dahmer replied that he was "lonely" and did not want his victims to leave him.

He claimed that he would approach potential victims in adult bookstores, shopping centers, or clubs, and then invite them back to his apartment where he would take their naked pictures in exchange for cash or alcohol.

Once the victim was knocked out, he would drug the beer before strangling and killing the victim. The ages of Dahmer's victims varied from 14 to 33. In Wisconsin, Dahmer was convicted of 15 counts of murder on February 15, 1992.

He was later found guilty of a second murder in his native Ohio. Due to a lack of evidence, the charges connecting him to other deaths were dismissed. With 15 obligatory life sentences to serve, he was transported to a jail in Wisconsin.

Dahmer was segregated from the other inmates throughout the first year of his sentence for his own safety. He was transferred to a maximum security prison in Portage in 1994 and given certain contact privileges with the other prisoners.

He was killed late on November 28, 1994, after being brutally beaten to death by Christopher Scarver, a fellow prisoner who claimed that God had told him to kill Jeffrey Dahmer.

Legal disputes over Dahmer's estate haven't ended despite his passing. His victims' families filed lawsuits against him, and they won settlements totaling millions of dollars.

Since then, those families have been attempting to take possession of Dahmer's apartment's belongings, which include the refrigerator where he kept the hearts of his victims and a 55-gallon tank he used to decompose bodies.

Fifteen

Albert Fish (The Gray Man)

Albert Fish initially went by the name Frank Howard. 18-year-old Edward Budd reached out to Frank Howard in response to Frank Howard's newspaper job posting. Edward Budd had a strong desire to succeed in life.

Budd received a job offer from Frank Howard. He (Frank Howard) told the tale of his six children and how his wife had abandoned them before stating that he would like to have Budd come work with him at his farm.

Howard even extended an employment offer to Willie, a friend of Budd's. Edward was eager to get a job and support his family.

A few days later, Howard intended to come get them so they could return to his farm and start working there.

When Howard didn't arrive, he gave a handwritten letter saying he'd get back to them in a few days. The family encouraged him to stay for lunch when he dropped by the next morning for a visit.

Howard noticed Gracie, Budd's younger sister, during his visit. He asked Gracie if she would like to accompany him, explaining that he had to attend a birthday party before he could take the boys to the farm.

The Budds permitted Gracie to join the celebration due to his courteous demeanor and amiable demeanor. Howard left that evening, and Gracie disappeared. Her disappearance was reported by the family to the local police, who then launched a search.

In part because Frank Howard didn't exist, no leads were found. A letter detailing the death and mutilation of young Gracie was delivered to the Bud family.

The handwriting on the note matched that on the initial note that was earlier sent to them. Another youngster disappeared while the investigation was underway and before the letter was received.

When Billy Gaffney, a four-year-old playing with Billy his neighbor, vanished, the three-year-old Billy said that "the boogey monster" had taken Billy Gaffney. The statement was not taken seriously by the police, who chose to ignore it.

Another youngster vanished not long after Billy Gaffney went missing. A feeble, elderly guy with grey hair was grumbling to himself as he strolled down the street. Eight-year-old Francis McDonnell and his mother were playing on the porch. His mother observed his uneasy demeanor but made no complaints.

Later that day, while Francis was having fun at the park, his pals noticed that he was accompanying an elderly man with grey hair into the woods. His family launched a search after learning that he was gone. Francis was discovered in the bushes, strangled with his suspenders and severely beaten.

The "grey man" was sought after, but despite extensive searches, he disappeared. Investigation revealed that the letter the Budd family received had a symbol of the New York Private Chauffeur's Benevolent Association (NYPCBA).

Each participant was obliged to get a handwriting test so that the results could be compared to the letters from Howard. A janitor came forward and admitted taking some paper and leaving it at his previous rooming home.

An elderly man who fit the description had resided there for two months and had just recently checked out, the landlady was able to confirm. Albert H. Fish was named as the previous occupant. Additionally, the landlady indicated that he wanted her to keep a letter that Albert's son would be sending.

The landlady informed the detectives that he would be coming to pick up his letter after they intercepted the mail at the post office. The primary investigator succeeded in apprehending Mr. Fish.

Law enforcement officials and psychologists heard a lot of confessions and testimonies. Mr. Fish explained his plan to kill Edward Budd and Willie by luring them to his farm.

However, as soon as he saw Gracie, he had a change of heart and yearned to murder her. He accompanied Gracie to the railway station where he bought her a one-way ticket. He took her to a house after the drive to the countryside.

At the residence, he instructed Gracie to wait outside while she selected flowers. He undressed completely and proceeded to the second level of the house. Gracie was startled by him when he beckoned for her to come upstairs and cried out for her mother. She was fatally choked by Mr. Fish.

He killed her, sliced up her body, and decapitated her. When he went, he brought the components with him, wrapped in newspaper. Due of his confession, police were able to find Gracie's remains.

Throughout his life, Albert Fish had numerous run-ins with the law. But each time, the accusations were dropped. He described how he tied up and battered Billy Gaffney as he went over the specifics of the crime. Even drinking his blood and using his body parts in a stew were admitted by him.

His behavior was not indicative of someone suffering from

psychosis. It was uncharacteristic of him to be so composed and quiet. He admitted that he desired to both inflict and experience pain.

He bullied kids, particularly guys, and took advantage of them. Additionally, he was driven to write and send vulgar letters. At least 29 needles were found, and an x-ray revealed that he had inserted them between his anus and scrotum.

The defense claimed that he was legally insane during the trial. To persuade the jurors that he was mentally ill, they provided several descriptions and testimonials. The jury, however, did not concur with this.

After a 10-day trial, he was determined to have a "psychopathic personality without a psychosis" and was convicted. He died by electrocution in 1936.

THANK YOU!

I sincerely hope you liked reading this book. If so, if you could spend a few minutes leaving me a review where you found this book.

Additionally, I'd want to invite you to join my email list for news, deals, and freebies on upcoming works! With upcoming freebies, I swear I'll make it worthwhile for you.
https://www.pearltruecrime.com/true-crime-free-book

Also, if you have a minute, follow me on Amazon One final thing. Readers like you have recommended a lot of the stories in the True Crime Cases series. If there's a true crime story you recall from the past that you haven't seen covered by other true crime sources, please tell me whatever facts you can recall and I will try to study it. I prefer to highlight stories that many true crime lovers haven't heard of. If you'd like to contact me, write me at: **support@pearltruecrime.com**

Thanks again,

Pearl Ndikum

About the Author

I have always been fascinated by serial killers wanting to know why they kill people and ways to prevent myself from becoming a victim.

In this book, I have compiled 15 true crime stories of the world's top true crime serial killers.

I examine their childhood, family, biography, and any relationships which may have prompted the killers to murder hundreds of people.

My aim is to educate the world about the various ways serial killers lure their victims and kill them so as to prevent anyone from falling victim in the future.

Thanks for reading.

You can connect with me on:

- https://www.pearltruecrime.com
- https://linktr.ee/pearltruecrime

Subscribe to my newsletter:

- https://www.pearltruecrime.com/true-crime-free-book

Also by Pearl Ndikum

Interested in more? The number of real crime case volumes I have is always growing. You may read the novels in any sequence and they are all available in Kindle, audiobook, and paperback, formats.

True Crime Cases Series

View the entire series on Amazon.

https://amazon.com/author/pearl-ndikum

FREE Bonus True Crime Stories

As a way to say thanks for reading this book, scan this QR code to get FREE Bonus True Crime Stories.

1) Open your phone camera

2) Point Camera at the QR Code

3) Tap the banner that appears.

Printed in Dunstable, United Kingdom

72649995R00047